Index to Techniques

Embellishments
pages 32-35

Stamping
pages 16-17, 50-51

Crackle Texture
*pages 6-9,
14-15, 20-21*

Stencil Texture
pages 12-13

Stamp on Canvas
pages 42-43

Paint
pages 4-5

Faux Background
pages 40-41

Faux Texture
pages 36-37

Stencil
pages 10-11, 22-23

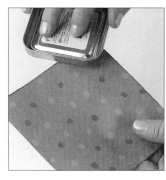

Age the Edges
pages 24-25

Collage
pages 30-31

Mixed Media
pages 48-49

Mixed Media
pages 28-29

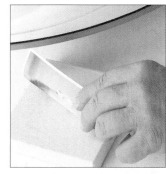

Photo Transfer
*pages 18-19, 26-27,
38-39*

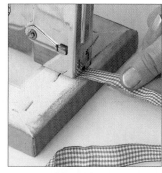

Attachments
pages 46-47

Fabric & Bows
pages 44-45

Faux Finish

One of the secrets to successful scrapbooking is great photography. Next time you are taking shots of the family at a gathering, take more than one. This layout is special because using three photos conveys far more information than just one. If your canvas is small, group three or four canvases together so you display this fall afternoon with all the richness and detail that you remember.

The faux finish on the rich gold paper mat was achieved by painting metallic copper over textured cardstock. You can get a similar effect by using a glaze and a combing technique, but the textured cardstock base provides a shortcut to this dramatic effect.

Choose colors that match your theme. Warm rust, tan and brown in the flower coordinate with the leaves in the photo and tie all the other colors together. The filigree corner stamp is also metallic copper and adds a bit of elegance to the corners, while barnyard red paint creates a bold title with foam stamps.

MATERIALS:

- 14" x 14" Canvas - *Canvas Concepts*
- Metallic Copper Ceramcoat Gleams acrylic paint - *Delta*
- Barnyard Red paint - *Plaid*
- Scarlet Color wash - *7gypsies*
- Tan Check paper - *Chatterbox*
- Rust cardstock - *Bazzill*
- Foam Stamps - *Making Memories*
- Ribbon - *May Arts*
- Photo Tape - *3L*
- Glue Dots - *Glue Dots International*
- Silk flower, foam brush

Family

by Krista Fernandez

INSTRUCTIONS:

1. Apply Scarlet Color wash to the bottom 6½" of the canvas with a foam brush. Let dry.
2. Stamp the title with Barnyard Red paint. Let dry.
3. Cut a Rust mat 6½" x 8½". Apply Metallic Copper to the mat with a foam brush for an iridescent finish.
4. Cut a Check mat 7½" x 9¾".
5. Mount a 5" x 7" photo to the mats and then to the canvas with Photo Tape.
6. Apply Metallic Copper to the corner stamp with a foam brush.
7. Stamp the corners as shown.
8. Tape the ribbon in place. Adhere the flower with Glue Dots.
9. Wrap ribbon around the corner of a 4" x 6" photo.
10. Tape the photos to the canvas.

1. Apply Color wash to the bottom of the canvas.

2. Apply Red paint to the foam stamps.

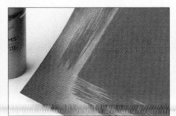

3. Apply Metallic Copper to the cardstock with a foam brush.

4. Adhere the flower with Glue Dots.

Crackle Technique

Crackle is not just for walls and furniture. The crackle mat in "Youth" provides an uncommon foundation for a rick-rack and button frame. Crackle can also provide unique coordinating corner accents. Try to think "outside the box" when you experiment with this fun medium. You can get some great textures and nearly any color you want.

Personalize the art with favorite quotes on transparency film, tags and pretty papers. Select the color palette from the subject's favorites. Remember that an initial can also add a special touch.

Scrapbooks often limit your work to the edge of the page. Presenting art on canvas gives you a lot of freedom to let items extend past the edges. Canvas also allows you more depth, so you can have a lot of fun choosing new embellishments.

Youth
by Krista Fernandez

MATERIALS:

- 12" x 12" Canvas - *Canvas Concepts*
- White acrylic paint - *Plaid*
- Mint Julep Green acrylic paint - *DecoArt*
- Crackle medium - *Delta*
- The Inker Black stamp pad - *Hero Arts*
- Patterned paper - *Autumn Leaves*
- Ribbon - *Offray*
- Rick-rack - *Wrights*
- Transparency - *Creative Imaginations*
- Rubber stamp - *Stampendous*
- LB Sheri and LB Marci - *CK Fonts*
- Brads, eyelet metal letter, metal rim tag - *Making Memories*
- Clay phrases - *Li'l Davis*
- Photo Tape - *3L*
- Glue Dots - *Glue Dots International*
- Staples, silk flowers, embossing powder

INSTRUCTIONS:

1. In the upper left corner of the canvas, paint a 7" x 9" area White. Let dry.
2. Apply an even coat of Crackle medium. Let dry 15-40 minutes until it becomes tacky.
3. Apply 1 light coat of Mint Julep Green paint, brushing in 1 direction. Let dry.
4. Edge the photo with White paint. Adhere the photo to the canvas.
5. Adhere the rick-rack around the photo, adding the initial tag and metal rim tag to the bottom rick-rack. Add Silver brads.
6. Add paper, ribbon and flowers to the corners as shown.
7. Print "keep true to the dreams of thy youth" by Longfellow on Green paper and edge it with Black ink. Adhere the message to the bottom of the page.
8. Position a Pink patterned paper under the transparency to highlight the word "youth". Adhere the Pink paper to the canvas. Staple folded ribbons to the right side of the transparency to attach it to the canvas.
9. Adhere flowers to the canvas.

1. Paint a White rectangle on the canvas.

2. Apply Crackle medium over the White paint.

3. Paint over the Crackle Medium with Mint Julep Green.

DREAMS Do Come TRUE

Crackle Technique

I was absolutely thrilled to find both fabric and papers that matched Cinderella's dress when designing this layout. That combination inspired this very simple, very elegant canvas. This project was a "dream come true" for my daughter's room. I hope it inspires you to scrapbook your dream and display it on a wall canvas.

Cinderella
by Michelle Tornay

MATERIALS:

- 14" x 14" Canvas - *Canvas Concepts*
- Paint (Baby Blue, White)
- Patterned paper - *Chatterbox*
- Cardstock - *Bazzill*
- Glass Knobs - *Provo Craft*
- Jigsaw Letters - *Making Memories*
- Paper Flowers - *Prima*
- Photo Tape - *3L*
- Scrappy Glue - *Magic Scraps*
- Fabric, heart ornaments, sewing machine, thread

INSTRUCTIONS:

1. Paint the canvas with Baby Blue. Let dry.
2. Drill 3 holes in the bottom of the canvas at 1", 7", and 13".
3. Screw crystal knobs into the drilled holes.
4. Cut 2 pieces each 3" x 4½" of Light Blue fabric and patterned paper.
5. Alternate the fabric and paper, making a piece 4½" x 12".
6. Zigzag stitch the seam where the fabric and paper meet. Straight stitch around three sides of the entire piece.
7. Cut one Blue cardstock strip ½" x 12" and sew a zigzag stitch down the center.
8. On a separate piece of 12" x 12" cardstock, adhere the sewn paper to the right hand side.
9. Paint the jigsaw letters White and Blue.
10. Adhere letters to make the words "Dreams Do Come True".
11. Adhere 3 flowers to bottom piece of patterned paper.
12. Adhere the 12" x 12" paper to the canvas.
13. Adhere the photo and Blue zigzag strip in place with Photo Tape.
14. Hang heart ornaments on the crystal knobs.

1. Paint the canvas Blue.

2. Attach knob to canvas.

3. Sew paper and fabric into a strip using a zigzag stitch.

4. Tape the paper/fabric strip to a sheet of 12" cardstock.

5. Paint the letters and glue them in place.

Stencil

"When I look at my daughter, I see myself, only better." What a beautiful, sensitive, positive sentiment to share with your child!

Art is so much more meaningful when it gives form to feelings. This canvas combines simple stenciling techniques with pretty papers and tulle to create a lovely presentation. Color-coordinated snaps, flowers and ribbons are the "just right" final touch.

Letter "A"
by Krista Fernandez

MATERIALS:

- 12" x 24" Canvas - *Canvas Concepts*
- Black paint - *DecoArt*
- Patterned paper, 4 Purple rivets, 2 small Purple nails - *Chatterbox*
- Patterned paper - *7gypsies*
- Transparency - *HP*
- Helvetica stencil - *Deja Views*
- Ribbon - *Offray, Scrap Wizard*
- Adler font - *www.scrapvillage.com*
- Diamond Glaze - *JudiKins*
- Photo Tape - *3L*
- Glue Dots - *Glue Dots International*
- Tulle, silk flowers, adhesive, staple gun, sewing machine

INSTRUCTIONS:

1. Paint the entire canvas with Black.
2. Cut 3 coordinating papers: 10" x 12", 7" x 12", and 5½" x 6¾".
3. Sew a zigzag or straight stitch around all 3 papers.
4. Use the stencil to cut out a large "A" from Black text paper. Trace the wrong side of the stencil on the back of the paper.
5. Evenly coat the "A" with Diamond Glaze. Let dry.
6. Adhere the "A" to the small paper and attach 4 rivets.
7. Adhere papers and photo to the canvas.
8. Cut 2 tags from coordinating papers and glue them together.
9. Print the title on a transparency.
10. Sew the transparency to the tags. Add ribbons and nails. Adhere tags to the canvas.
11. Cut 2 strips of tulle 2¼" x 30".
12. Tie knots randomly along the tulle strips.
13. Staple the ends of the tulle to the back of the canvas.
14. Adhere flowers to the tulle.

1. Paint the canvas Black.

2. Trace the reverse of the stencil on the back of the paper.

3. Coat the letter with Diamond Glaze.

4. Staple tulle to the back of the canvas.

1. Place the stencil on the small canvas and apply Almond Texture Magic. Let dry.

2. Ink the image with Soft Wheat.

3. Center the small canvas and place petals around it.

4. Cover the petals with tulle.

5. Staple the tulle to the back of the canvas frame.

Stenciling

A young couple's nuptials are fraught with images — wedding white, rose petals, veils, delicate moments, breathless expectations. Celebrate the happiest day of your lives with a frame as resplendent as your love. White silk petals sprinkle onto this frame, surrounding this newly wed couple. Bridal veil tulle holds these airy flowers in place, creating the perfect frame for this absolutely gorgeous wedding photo. The stenciled pattern mimics the fancy embroidery in the bridal gown and groom's shirt.

Make this canvas as a stand-alone piece, or accompany it with smaller photos that tell the whole story of your most special day.

Wedding Portrait
by Emelyn Magpoc

MATERIALS:

- One 8" x 12" Canvas and one 16" x 16" Natural finish Canvas - *Canvas Concepts*
- Almond Texture Magic, Texture Magic Spreader, Flower stencil - *Delta*
- Coffee Bean Brilliance ink - *Tsukineko*
- Soft Wheat ink - *Memories*
- White Rose Petals - *Precious Petals*
- Cream tulle - *Modern Romance*
- Photo Tape - *3L*
- Staple gun

INSTRUCTIONS:

1. Place the stencil near the bottom of the small canvas.
2. Generously apply Almond Texture Magic over the stencil.
3. Spread the Texture Magic completely over the stencil image.
4. Carefully remove the stencil, maintaining the raised image. Let dry.
5. Smear Texture Magic over the edges of the canvas. Let dry.
6. Ink the edges and raised image with Soft Wheat.
7. Ink the large canvas with Coffee Bean, making the edges darker than the center.
8. Center the small canvas over the larger canvas.
9. Place rose petals along the sides of the small canvas to form a frame.
10. Carefully remove the small canvas without disturbing the petals.
11. Place tulle over the rose petals, leaving a lot of tulle to fold over to the back.
12. Center the small canvas over the tulle.
13. Hold everything in place and carefully flip it over.
14. Staple the tulle to the back of the frame.
15. Staple the small canvas in place.
16. Tape the photo to the canvas.

uNLock yOur

IMAGINATION

Crackle Technique

When it comes to trains, my son has a one-track mind. He loves them. The wood puzzle track is the perfect complement for this great photo, and inspired the wood tone in the crackle I used to cover the small canvas.

Search your child's toy box for items that complement your art and stimulate ideas. Children have such a wonderfully simple way of looking at the world. I believe this canvas captures that sentiment.

Unlock Your Imagination
by Emelyn Magpoc

MATERIALS:

- One 8" x 8" Canvas, one 16" x 16" Natural finish Canvas - *Canvas Concepts*
- Paint (Spice Brown, Trail Tan) - *Delta*
- Regency Blue paint - *Plaid* Apple Barrel
- Crackle medium - *Plaid* Folk Art
- Nick Bantock Van Dyke Brown ink - *Ranger*
- Train tracks - *Thomas the Tank Engine*
- Rub-Ons, Fabric letters - *Making Memories*
- Photo Tape - *3L*
- Liquid Nails - *Macco Adhesives*
- Staple gun

INSTRUCTIONS:

1. Paint both canvases with Spice Brown. Let dry.
2. Paint the large canvas with Regency Blue. Let dry.
3. Paint the small canvas with Crackle Medium. Let dry.
4. Paint the small canvas with Trail Tan. Let dry.
5. Ink the edges of both canvases.
6. Adhere the train tracks with Liquid Nails.
7. Ink the train tracks.
8. Staple the small canvas to the large canvas.
9. Adhere Rub-Ons and fabric letters to create the title.
10. Adhere the photo to the small canvas with Photo Tape.

1. Paint the large canvas Brown.

2. Paint Regency Blue over the Brown on the large canvas.

3. Paint the small canvas with Crackle Medium.

4. Paint the small canvas with Trail Tan.

5. Ink the edges of the canvas.

Stamping

Add color to a canvas with background papers, rubber stamps and small accents in richly vibrant earth tones when your photograph is black and white.

Does your canvas need that last final touch in the corner to make it perfect? Look at the elegant effect achieved by using a filigree stamp.

Add a bit of texture and movement by joining background papers with a zigzag stitch on your sewing machine, and by attaching silk flowers to the canvas. They have the same shape as her tiny earrings and add depth and beauty to this layout.

Angel
by Michelle Tornay

MATERIALS:

- 16" x 16" Canvas - *Canvas Concepts*
- Acrylic paint (Linen, Brown) - *Plaid* Folk Art
- Nick Bantock Van Dyke Brown ink - *Ranger*
- Patterned paper (Brown Diamonds, Red Script, Brown words) - *7gypsies*
- Cardstock - *Bazzill*
- Foam stamps and Jigsaw Letters - *Making Memories*
- Photo Tape - *3L*
- Scrappy Glue - *Magic Scraps*
- Silk flowers, Tan ribbon, sewing machine, thread, foam brush, adhesive

INSTRUCTIONS:

1. Paint the canvas with Linen. Let it dry.
2. Ink the edges of canvas.
3. Stamp the canvas corners with a foam stamp and Brown paint.
4. Paint the jigsaw letters.
5. Cut 2 strips of each the Red Script paper and the Brown words paper 3" x 4" and sew them together with a zigzag stitch to make a 4" x 12" strip.
6. Adhere jigsaw letters and flowers to the right-hand side of the canvas.
7. Tape the 12" x 12" Diamonds paper to the upper left-hand side of the canvas.
8. Tape the sewn paper below the Diamonds paper.
9. Cut an 8" square of Red Script paper and zigzag stitch around the top and left side.
10. Adhere the Red Script to the canvas.
11. Wrap a ribbon around the bottom of the photo and attach a flower.
12. Adhere the photo in place.

1. Paint the canvas Linen.

2. Ink the edges of the canvas.

3. Paint the stamp and stamp the canvas.

4. Sew the 3" x 4" papers together into a strip.

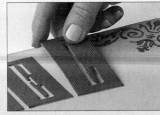

5. Adhere Jigsaw letters to canvas with Photo Tape.

6. Tape the Diamond paper in place.

7. Tape the sewn strip in place.

Photo Transfer

You are going to be surprised at how easy it is to transfer a photo directly to canvas. This technique opens a world of possibilities for creating both simple and collaged artwork.

Also, look at the easy method for putting these pieces together - tied ribbons! Eye screws are inexpensive and easily available. And there is a stunning array of ribbons and fibers on the market today. Your most difficult decision may be which fiber or ribbon you like best.

"This artwork needs ....no, not that. Something else...I'll know it when I see it!" Next time you find yourself thinking this, visit your local craft store and take a walk down the floral aisle. Picture the spray without the stems and leaves. You may find the "just right" bit of flowery "something" that you have been looking for.

Family of Love

by Suzy West

MATERIALS:

- Eleven 4" x 4" and two 4" x 8" Canvases - *Canvas Concepts*
- Decorative paper - *Chatterbox*
- Letters, Photo Corners - *Making Memories*
- Flowers - *JoAnn Fabrics*
- Eye Hooks, Photo Transfers - *Canvas Concepts*
- Ribbon - *May Arts*
- Scrappy Glue - *Magic Scraps*
- Photo Tape - *3L*

INSTRUCTIONS:

For Canvases with photos:
1. Scan in and print your pictures onto photo transfer paper.
2. Cut them to size.
3. Iron them onto the canvases following manufacturer's directions. Let the transfer sit until it's completely cool.

For canvases without photos:
4. Cut papers to size and ink the edges.
5. Adhere papers to the canvases.
6. Adhere flowers on top of pattern paper.

For 4" x 8" canvases:
7. Computer print the title.
8. Cut papers to size and adhere them to the canvases.
9. Paint the letters and adhere them to the canvas.
10. Adhere the metal letters and photo corners.

Finishing all canvases:
11. Ink the edges of all canvases.

Connecting the canvases:
12. Mark the positions for the eye hooks.
13. Screw eye hooks into the canvas
14. Tie the screw hooks together with ribbon.

1. Iron photo onto canvas.

2. Mark position for screw eyes.

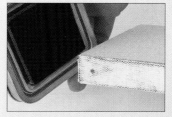

3. Ink the canvas edges Brown.

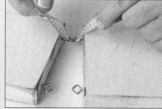

4. Tie canvases together with ribbon.

Crackle Technique

Calling all cowboys, cowgirls, and rodeo wanna-be's! Lasso a great place to hang your hat when you add a hook to the bottom of this wild west canvas. Western themed papers make it so easy to cover the space, and you can use any photo collection that reflects the western mystique.

For example, this canvas would be a fun place for those shots of you learning to "boot scoot". Did you keep the napkin from that historic saloon? Adding ephemera makes your art more fun to admire.

Even if you've never been out west, you can collect western postcards and use this canvas to organize your display. You can also collect images of the places you would like to go.

If you have tickets and memorabilia from the rodeo, don't hide them away in a scrapbook. Tack them onto this canvas with a small piece of barbed wire or an aged scrap of wood. The dimensional possibilities of canvas are limitless.

Cowboy

by Michelle Tornay

MATERIALS:

- One 8" x 12" and one 12" x 24" Canvas - *Canvas Concepts*
- Linen acrylic paint - *Plaid* Folk Art
- Plasti-kote Gold Crackle Base and White Top Coat - *Plasti-Kote Co., Inc.*
- Nick Bantock Van Dyke Brown ink - *Ranger*
- Paper (Cowboy, Bandana) - *K&Company*
- Cardstock - *Bazzill*
- Photo Tape - *3L*
- Scrappy Glue - *Magic Scraps*
- Hook, wooden letter

INSTRUCTIONS:

1. Spray paint the 8" x 12" canvas with Gold Crackle Base.
2. Spray White Crackle Top Coat over the Gold canvas following the manufacturer's instructions.
3. Cut the following:
   Cowboy paper: 3 strips 2" x 5¼", 2 strips 2" x 12";
   Bandana paper: 3 strips 2" x 5¼", 1 strip 7½" x 12", 1 strip 4" x 12";
   Brown cardstock: 4 strips ½" x 12".
4. Ink the wooden letters and the edges of all cut papers.
5. Paint the edges of the large canvas. Let dry.
6. Adhere the papers and photos to the canvas.
7. Adhere the letters "Cowboy" and "H" in place.
8. Attach the hook to the bottom frame of the canvas.

1. Spray Crackle onto the canvas.

2. Ink the wooden letters.

3. Paint the edge of the large canvas Linen.

4. Adhere paper to canvas.

5. Adhere letters to canvas.

6. Attach hook in place.

Thank goodness *for*

LITTLE Girls

Stenciling

You can make your own stencil letters! Just print out the size and font you desire, in the color that you need, and cut them out with a pair of scissors or a craft knife. Computer printing allows you to custom design your own letters, and saves you money!

"Little Girls" uses both purchased stencil letters and computer printed ones. You can also use die-cut stencil letters for a different look.

Little Girls
by Suzy West

MATERIALS:

- One 4" x 8", one 4" x 4", and one 14" x 14" Canvas - *Canvas Concepts*
- Acrylic paint (Burnt Orange, Black) paint - *Making Memories*
- Mod Podge - *Plaid*
- Rust ink
- Papers - *Scenic Route Papers*
- Ribbons - *May Arts*
- Stencils - *Making Memories*
- Wood Letters - *Li'l Davis Designs*
- Photo Tape - *3L*
- Scrappy Glue - *Magic Scraps*
- Flowers

INSTRUCTIONS:

1. Paint all canvases Orange. Let dry.

Large Canvas:

2. Paint the stencil letters "for" with Black.
3. Ink and adhere your papers to the canvas.
4. Adhere photos.
5. Computer print the words "Thank goodness" and cut them out.
6. Glue "Thank goodness" in place.
7. Ink the edges of the canvases with Rust.
8. Mod Podge the whole thing. Let dry.
9. Add ribbon and a flower to the top right of the canvas.

4" x 8" Canvas:

10. Paint the stencil letters "girls" and the wood letters. Let dry.
11. Ink the letter edges with Rust.
12. Adhere papers to the canvas.
13. Mod Podge the whole canvas.
14. Adhere a flower and ribbon.

4" Canvas:

15. Cut photo to fit the canvas.
16. Adhere photo.
17. Apply Mod Podge all over the canvas.

1. Paint canvases Burnt Orange.

2. Paint stencil letters Black.

3. Ink the edges of the paper.

4. Adhere papers to the canvas.

5. Cut out letters.

6. Mod Podge entire project.

Mixed Media

Fall Fun really lives up to its name. Using purchased metal and painted wood accents takes the work out of putting this awesome autumnal layout together.

Enlarge your photo to fit the canvas to establish a fabulous focal point that will enrich any fall decor. This rich artwork would also make a great year-round addition to your garden or sunroom.

Screw eyes hold the project together and make it easy to arrange the components in a pleasing manner.

If you are looking for a quick and easy project to fill a sunny afternoon, this is the layout for you. And for those of you who can't decide which embellishments you like best, buy them all. Then make extra complementary canvas pieces. You can display them as a set on the same wall or spread the theme about the room.

Fall Fun
by Suzy West

MATERIALS:

- Two 6" x 6" and one 8" x 12" Canvases - *Canvas Concepts*
- Green paint - *Delta*
- Nick Bantock Van Dyke Brown ink - *Ranger*
- Patterned paper - *Chatterbox*
- 4 screw eyes - *Canvas Concepts*
- Photo Tape - *3L*
- Metal embellishments, wood scarecrow

INSTRUCTIONS:

1. Paint the small canvases Green. Paint only the edges of the large canvas. Let dry.
2. Glue the metal embellishment to a small canvas.
3. Cut a patterned paper 5" x 5" and ink the edges with Brown.
4. Tape the paper to a small canvas.
5. Adhere the scarecrow to the paper.
6. Measure and mark the screw eye placement.
7. Add screw eyes to your canvases.
8. Add photo to 8" x 12" canvas.
9. Connect all the pieces.

1. Paint the canvases Green.

2. Ink the edges of the canvas.

3. Ink the edges of the paper.

4. Tape the scarecrow to the canvas.

5. Paint the hooks Brown.

6. Screw in the screw eyes.

Photo Transfer

Photo transfer gives you a lot of freedom to do groupings of any size. These little canvases are perfect for enlarging face shots. Next time you get one of those little wallet size photos, consider enlarging it so you can make your own, very "together" set of canvas art.

2Gether
by Krista Fernandez

MATERIALS:

- Two 8" x 8", three 4" x 4", one 4" x 8" Canvases - *Canvas Concepts*
- Pastel Peach Color Wash - *7gypsies*
- Photo transfer, screw eyes, Canvas Clips - *Canvas Concepts*
- Polka Dots paper, Light Blue cardstock - *SEI*
- Orange Text paper - *Autumn Leaves*
- Blue Script paper - *Daisy D*
- Ribbon (Blue Gingham, Orange Sheer) - *Offray*
- Wide Light Blue ribbon - *Garden Gate Designs*
- Foam alphabet stamps, Monarch acrylic paint - *Making Memories*
- Stencil - *X-Acto*
- Glue Dots - *Glue Dots International*
- Photo Tape - *3L*
- Silk flowers, staple gun, hole punch

INSTRUCTIONS:

1. Staple the 8" canvases together on the front and back seams.
2. Paint the edges of all canvases with Pastel Peach Color Wash. Let dry.
3. Cut 3 strips of paper 5½" x 8". Adhere them together.
4. Machine stitch the seams where the papers meet. Adhere papers to the canvases.
5. Transfer photos onto the 4" canvases following manufacturer's directions.
6. Paint the edges of the 4" canvases Monarch. Adhere the 4" canvases in place.
7. Stamp the title on a Light Blue cardstock with Monarch paint. Let dry.
8. Add a trim of coordinating patterned paper.
9. Sew a zigzag stitch across the trim. Adhere title to the canvas.
10. Punch holes in a number stencil. Attach ribbon with a Lark's Head knot.
11. Adhere the stencil and flower to the canvas.
12. Screw 2 screw eyes into the top of the title canvas.
13. Thread a ribbon through the eyes to create a hanger.
14. Hang the long canvas from the title canvas using Canvas Clips.

1. Staple the canvases together.

2. Paint the edges of all canvases with Pastel Peach Color Wash.

3. Copy photos onto photo transfer paper. Color photos can be photocopied in black and white.

4. Place photo transfer on canvas surface.

5. Iron photo transfer according to manufacturer's directions.

Mixed Media

Create a dramatic presentation of the dreamy demeanors, adventurous attitudes, and sweet expressions of your child with this "Mackenzie" layout. Perfect for enhancing a little girl's room, the lovely lavender background and accents bring out the colors in the photographs and give this artwork a delicate, feminine look that is very pleasing to the eye.

If you're just looking for a charming departure from the usual photo mat, check out this wonderful waffle fabric and matboard. The circular photo slots provide a dimensional space to hold those special small photos as well as expressive accents.

Mackenzie
by Michelle Tornay

MATERIALS:

- One 14" x 14" and two 6" x 6" Canvases - *Canvas Concepts*
- Lilac Purple paint - *Plaid* Folk Art
- 12" x 12" Scrap Mat, Patterned paper - *K&Company*
- Wood "3" and "M" - *Walnut Hollow*
- Real Life Keepsake Pocket - *Pebbles*
- Ribbon - *Offray*
- Key Charm - *K&Company*
- Canvas phrase - *All My Memories*
- Canvas Words - *Li'l Davis*
- Epoxy stickers - *Creative Imaginations*
- Blossoms and Daisy trim - *Making Memories*
- Letter stickers - *me & my BiG ideas*
- 2 Photo Clips - *Canvas Concepts*
- Scrappy Glue - *Magic Scraps*
- Photo Tape - *3L*
- Lavender waffle weave fabric

INSTRUCTIONS:

1. Paint all canvases Lilac. Let dry.
2. Tape 12" x 12" paper behind the Scrap Mat.
3. Embellish the Scrap Mat.
4. Cut a Lavender fabric mat for each photo. Wrap one edge of the fabric around the Scrap Mat and adhere it in place with Photo Tape.
5. Adhere sticker letters to the fabric to spell out the name.
6. Tie a ribbon and key around the mat.
7. Adhere scrap mat to the 14" canvas.
8. Adhere Daisy trim, patterned paper, and photos to each small canvas.
9. Adhere a ribbon to the Photo Clip with Photo Tape.
10. Attach the Canvas Clips.

1. Paint canvases Lilac.

2. Tie the ribbon and key around the Scrap Mat.

3. Attach embellished mat to the large canvas.

4. Tape ribbon to the Canvas Clips.

1. Paint the sides of the canvases Blue.

2. Frame the photo with Gingham ribbon.

3. Cut a 4½" window in the frame.

4. Adhere fabric and paper to the frame.

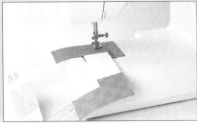

5. Stitch around the edges of the frame.

Fabric

This project began as a tactile challenge. I wanted to see how many different textures I could get to work harmoniously with a masculine theme. The result was a sweet success that contrasts the "rough and tumble" expectations we have of boys with the tender sensitivity that so often catches us by surprise.

Even Charles Schulz's 'Linus' had his favorite blanket. I chose my color palette from my cousin's favorite quilt, and tried to recreate the effect of patchwork in the frame design. I think quilted designs give warmth to a project.

I hope this work ignites your desire to experiment with combining papers, transparencies, and all kinds of fabrics.

Moments
by Krista Fernandez

MATERIALS:

- Two 8" x 8" Canvases - *Canvas Concepts*
- Light Periwinkle acrylic paint - *Plaid*
- Mod Podge - *Plaid*
- Patterned paper, cardstock, and transparency - *K&Company*
- 2 eye screws, 2 Canvas Clips - *Canvas Concepts*
- Page Pebble, Rub-Ons - *Making Memories*
- Tile - *Junkitz*
- Ribbon (Narrow Blue Sheer, Narrow Gingham) - *Offray*
- Wide Gingham ribbon - *Michaels*
- Wide Blue sheer ribbon - *Morex Corp.*
- Rick-rack - *Wrights*
- Address alphabet stickers - *Chatterbox*
- Photo Tape - *3L*
- Burlap, eyelet fabric, waffle fabric, hammer, nail, pliers

INSTRUCTIONS:

1. Paint the sides of both canvases with Light Periwinkle Blue. Let dry.
2. Adhere a 4" x 4" photo to the center of the canvas.
3. Frame the photo with gingham ribbon.
4. Cut two 8" squares of heavy cardstock.
5. Cut a 4½" square window in the center of the 8" square.
6. Cover the frame with fabrics, papers, and transparencies.
7. Add Rub-Ons to the burlap. Seal with a light coat of Mod Podge.
8. Machine stitch around all edges of the frame.
9. Adhere the frame to the canvas.
10. Mark the place you want your eye screws. Make a starter hole by hammering in a nail, then remove the nail with pliers. Twist the eye screws in place.
11. Thread a ribbon through the eye screws for hanging.
12. Attach the second canvas with Canvas Clips.

Hardware

The combination of canvas and hardware allows a simple towel hanger to become an integral part of photographic art. "Bath Time Buddies" is a good example of practical and useful home decor.

1. Paint both canvases Blue.

2. Attach photo to canvas.

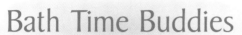

Bath Time Buddies
by Emelyn Magpoc

MATERIALS:

- One 4" x 8" and one 12" x 12" Canvases - *Canvas Concepts*
- Blue acrylic paint - *DecoArt* Americana
- Nick Bantock Blue ink - *Ranger*
- Patterned paper - *SEI*
- Cardstock (Blue, White) - *Bazzill*
- Metal letters - *Making Memories*
- 2 Canvas Clips - *Canvas Concepts*
- Chipboard letters - *Li'l Davis*
- 8" Yellow dotted ribbon - *The Weathered Door*
- Diamond Glaze - *JudiKins*
- Photo tape - *3L*
- Railboard hook kit - *Target*
- Door knobs, drill

3. Ink the edges of the Railboard.

4. Drill holes for door knobs.

INSTRUCTIONS:

1. Paint both canvases with 2 coats of Blue. Let dry.

Title Canvas:

2. Cut the following: Paper 4" x 8"; Blue cardstock 2" x 7½"; White cardstock 1" x 7".
3. Ink paper and cardstock with Blue.
4. Adhere patterned paper to the 4" x 8" canvas.
5. Adhere an 8" Yellow dotted ribbon to the top of the Blue cardstock.
6. Adhere White cardstock below the Yellow ribbon.
7. Adhere the metal letters to the White cardstock with Diamond Glaze.
8. Adhere chipboard letters below the White cardstock with Diamond Glaze.

Large Canvas:

9. Ink the edges of 12" x 12" patterned paper with Blue.
10. Adhere patterned paper to the canvas.
11. Cut Blue cardstock 7½" x 10" and ink the edges Blue.
12. Adhere cardstock to the canvas.
13. Adhere 6¾" x 9½" photo to cardstock.
14. Ink edges of the White block from the railboard kit.
15. Drill holes for the door knobs.
16. Attach door knobs to the railboard.
17. Attach railboard to the canvas.
18. Attach canvases with Canvas Clips.

5. Attach the doorknobs

6. Add letters to the title.

Hardware

Create a special place to display and store your baby's precious keepsakes. This "Treasures" box holds baby's shoes, diaper pins, hairbrush and sweet yellow ducky. Placing a photo of your child in the top frame gives "treasures" a double meaning.

A little bit of hardware allows you to turn a shadowbox into a real box. A square canvas forms the top and bottom of this sweet storage container.

Treasure Box
by Suzy West

MATERIALS:

- Two 8" x 8" Canvases - *Canvas Concepts*
- Paints (Tan, Green, Burnt Orange) - *American Crafts, Making Memories*
- Mod Podge - *Plaid*
- Pattern Paper - *Chatterbox*
- Wood Letters - *Li'l Davis*
- Ribbon - *May Arts*
- Metal Word - *Karen Foster*
- Metal Corners - *Making Memories*
- Wood Shadowbox - *JoAnn Fabrics*
- Wood Frame - *Ikea*
- Hinges, Adhesive - *Canvas Concepts*
- Scrappy Glue - *Magic Scraps*

INSTRUCTIONS:

1. Paint canvases Green, wood shadowbox Tan, and photo frame Orange. Let dry.

Lid:

2. Cut paper to size and adhere to both sides of the canvas.
3. Tie a ribbon on your frame. Place a photo in the frame. Adhere frame to the canvas.
4. Position letters on the top of the canvas. Adhere the letters in place.
5. Adhere the metal corners and metal word "treasures".

Box:

6. Place the lid on top of the wood box.
7. Adhere the bottom canvas to the bottom of the box.
8. Screw the hinges into the canvas and the box.
9. Mod Podge the entire project.

1. Paint the canvas Green.

2. Adhere Striped paper to the front of the canvas.

3. Adhere paper to the back of the canvas.

4. Set the box on the bottom canvas.

5. Hinge the lid to the box.

1. Paint all canvases Blue.

2. Attach the canvases together with clips.

3. Apply Sandstones Texture Medium. Let dry.

4. Adhere seashells with hot glue.

5. Clean off the ridges of the corrugated cardboard.

6. Ink the cardboard ridges with Coffee Bean.

Faux Finish

The beach cares not for life's demands.
Horizon of my mind is clear.
We lightly walk o'er snow white sands.
We've waited to do this all year!

Recreate the sparkling white sands of your favorite oceanside vacation spot with this fabulous faux technique. You even get the ripples left by the waves. And what do you always find on the beach? Seashells, of course. This collection is stunning against the sand.

Continue that "at the beach" feeling with a bit of gauze behind a corrugated paper for the title. It will remind you of driftwood and sun-bleached fishing net. A bit of raveled twine provides the perfect finishing touch.

MATERIALS:

- Two 8" x 8" and one 8" x 12" Canvases - *Canvas Concepts*
- Cape Cod Blue paint - *Delta*
- Textured Sandstones - *DecoArt*
- Coffee Bean Brilliance ink - *Tsukineko*
- Canvas clips - *Canvas Concepts*
- Mailbox Letters - *Making Memories*
- Diamond Glaze - *JudiKins*
- Photo Tape - *3L*
- Seashells, corrugated cardboard, twine, gauze, drinking straw, hot glue gun

Beach Fun
by Emelyn Magpoc

INSTRUCTIONS:

1. Paint all canvases Cape Cod Blue.
2. Attach canvases together with clips.
3. Use a straw to apply Sandstones Texture Medium to the bottom of the canvases. Let dry.
4. Adhere seashells with hot glue.
5. Tear off the top layer of the cardboard and clean off the grooves to expose the ridges.
6. Ink the cardboard with Coffee Bean.
7. Tie twine to the edges of the cardboard photo mat.
8. Mat photos on cardboard with Photo Tape.
9. Adhere mailbox letters to the cardboard to make the title.
10. Tie twine to the bottom corners of the title box.
11. Adhere photo mats to the small canvas with Diamond Glaze.
12. Adhere gauze and title box to the large canvas with Diamond Glaze.

1. Paint edges of canvases.

2. Ink the painted wooden letters.

3. Zigzag around the edge of the frames and squares.

4. Tape the Blue squares to the center of the 6" squares.

5. Adhere letters to the Blue squares.

6. Iron photo transfer onto canvas following manufacturer's directions.

7. Hook the canvases together.

8. Tie a ribbon around the linked eye hooks.

Photo Transfer

Any of your favorite papers will work well with transferred photos. Once you begin this technique, you won't want to stop. That's how this layout ended up with a dozen canvases. I just started transferring the photos I liked best, then I filled in the holes. The wonderful thing about this technique is that it works for any length of name and any number of photos. This looks like a large project, but if you cut all the paper frames at once, this will go together very quickly.

"Daniel" captures his personality with photos that show many different moods. You can also use this format to display a progression of photos for a charming "growing up" layout.

Tied ribbons and eye screws make connecting the components inexpensive and simple. The letters that spell out "Daniel" are found in most home improvement stores in the mailbox department.

Daniel

by Michelle Tornay

MATERIALS:

- Twelve 6" x 6" Canvases - *Canvas Concepts*
- Paint (Wedgewood Blue, Primary Yellow) - *Delta*
- Nick Bantock Van Dyke Brown ink - *Ranger*
- Patterned paper - *Basic Grey*
- Blue cardstock - *Bazzill*
- 32 Eye Hooks - *Canvas Concepts*
- Photo Transfer Paper - *Canvas Concepts*
- Photo Tape - *3L*
- Scrappy Glue - *Magic Scraps*
- 5⅓ yards Blue ribbon ⅝" wide, wooden letters, pliers, sewing machine, thread

INSTRUCTIONS:

1. Paint the edges of all 12 canvases with Wedgewood Blue. Let dry.
2. Paint the wooden letters Yellow. Let dry.
3. Cut 12 squares 6" x 6" from patterned paper.
4. Cut a 4" x 4" window in the center of 6 of the squares.
5. Cut 6 Blue cardstock 4" squares.
6. On the patterned paper frames, sew a zigzag stitch around the outer edge. Sew a straight stitch around the windows.
7. Sew a straight stitch around the edge of the Blue squares.
8. Ink around all sewn edges.
9. Adhere 6 squares to the canvases.
10. Adhere the 4" squares to the center of the 6" squares.
11. Ink the wooden letters.
12. Adhere wooden letters to the Blue squares.
13. Copy 6 photos 4" x 4" onto the photo transfer paper.
14. Iron photos onto canvases following manufacturer's instructions.
15. Adhere paper frames to the photo transferred canvases.
16. Screw eye hooks in place by twisting them into the wooden frame of the canvas.
17. Link top and bottom of canvases together alternating letters and photo transfers.
18. Close eye hooks with pliers.
19. Cut 32 strips of ribbon 6" long.
20. Tie ribbons around linked eye hooks.

1. Sponge paint mixture onto canvases.

2. Mark the holes for the hinges.

3. Adhere sewn paper to chipboard.

4. Ink the edges of the paper/chipboard.

5. Cut a hole in the middle of the center canvas.

6. Adhere the clock face to the wood.

7. Assemble the clockworks from the back of the canvas.

8. Assemble the clock hands from the front.

 *Faux Finish*

When you need a soft, subtle background pattern on your canvas, consider this faux technique. It is very simple to do and the results can be breathtaking.

Pretty papers edged with zigzag stitch form the mats for all three canvases and the borders are edged with satin ribbon tied with a charm. By the way, the clock is real, so this art serves double duty. Put it on a mantle in the living room to proclaim your relationship as a timeless treasure.

Timeless Love is elegant canvas art that is not complicated or difficult to produce. It is simply lovely.

 Timeless Love
by Michelle Tornay

MATERIALS:

- Three 8" x 8" Canvases - *Canvas Concepts*
- Acrylic paint (Italian Sage, Parchment) - *Plaid Folk Art*
- Faux Paint Medium - *Plaid*
- Nick Bantock Van Dyke Brown ink - *Ranger*
- Patterned paper - *Autumn Leaves*
- 4 hinges - *Canvas Concepts*
- Clock Kit - *Walnut Hollow*
- Ribbon - *Offray*
- Key and Lock Charms - *K&Company*
- Letter stickers - *me and my BiG ideas*
- Photo Tape - *3L*
- Scrappy Glue - *Magic Scraps*
- Wood circle to fit clock, chipboard, large artist sponge, drill, sewing machine, thread

INSTRUCTIONS:

1. Use a large artist sponge to apply a mixture of equal parts Italian Sage paint and Faux paint medium to all 3 canvases.
2. Ink the edges of all of 3 canvases.
3. Hinge the canvases together 1" from the top and bottom.
4. Cut the following from patterned papers and chipboard: Two 6" x 7½", one 6" square.
5. Sew a zigzag stitch around each paper.
6. Adhere chipboard to the back of each paper and ink the edges.
7. Apply photo and letter stickers to each 6" x 7½" piece.
8. Adhere patterned paper backed with chipboard to the canvases.
9. Paint the wood circle with Parchment.
10. Drill a hole in the middle of the wood circle.
11. Ink the edges of the wood circle.
12. Cut a piece of patterned paper to fit the center of the wood circle.
13. Ink the edges of the paper.
14. Adhere the paper to the wood.
15. Punch a small hole in the middle of the center canvas.
16. Tie ribbons and charms around the edge of the two outer canvases.
17. Adhere the wood circle to the middle of the center canvas.
18. Adhere the face of the clock to the wood circle.
19. Add clock mechanism and hands following the manufacturer's instructions.

Stamping

The next time you can't find the perfect paper to cover a canvas, consider your rubber stamp collection. You can fashion stunning backgrounds just by repeating one design in the same color, or collage a group of stamps into an eclectic array of color and image. Stamping opens a door to new texture, line, image and color that will enrich your art and increase the fun you have creating it.

Astonishing use of color and motif captures the eye and draw one's attention right into this charming little girl's face. You, too, can make canvas art that no one will be able to resist. Choose your most beautiful photograph, and base your color choice on the photo. Choose a motif related to the image. For example, in "One" the flowers in the lei led to the choice of rubber stamp and the silk flowers. Beautiful ribbons complement the delicate pink colors in the flowers and photograph.

One
by Emelyn Magpoc

MATERIALS:
- One 8" x 12", one 14" x 14", and three 4" x 4" Canvases - *Canvas Concepts*
- Acrylic paint (Green, Pink, White) - *Delta*
- Screw eyes - *Canvas Concepts*
- Foam paisley stamp - *Making Memories*
- Wooden letters, ribbon, flowers - *Michael's*
- Photo tape - *3L*
- Diamond Glaze - *JudiKins*
- Staple gun, hot glue gun

INSTRUCTIONS:
1. Paint the 14" and the 4" canvases Green. Let dry.
2. Paint the front edge of the 4" canvases White. Let dry.
3. Paint the 8" x 12" canvas Pink. Let dry.
4. Paint the letters Pink. Let dry.
5. Paint the letters White. Let dry.

Large Canvas
6. Stamp the paisleys with White paint. Let dry.
7. Tape the photo to the Pink canvas.
8. Staple the Pink canvas to the 14" canvas from the back.
9. Hot glue the flowers in place.

Hanging Canvases
10. Tie a ribbon on each letter, securing a flower stem.
11. Adhere the letter to the 4" canvas with Diamond Glaze.
12. Attach screw eyes to the corner of the 4" canvases and the bottom of the 14" canvas.
13. Use ribbon to connect the 4" canvases to the 14" canvas.

1. Paint canvases Green.

2. Stamp the large canvas.

3. Edge small canvases with White.

4. Paint over the Pink letter with White.

5. Staple the Pink canvas to the Green canvas.

6. Tie the small canvases to the large one with ribbon.

Fabric

I had been saving this photo for a long time. When I heard the song "I hope you dance", I was inspired to dig out my daughter's old ballet slippers and tutu. The result is a really fun decoration for her room that celebrates a very special time in our lives.

The joy on her face when she is dancing is so moving that I want to see it every day. I hope this canvas encourages you to not only pull some of those favorite scrapbook memories onto canvas, but also think of fabric in new and exciting ways. I love the texture created by covering the small canvas with tulle. Even if you don't sew, taking a walk through your local fabric store can invigorate your perception of what will enhance your scrapbooking adventure.

Ballerina Dancer
by Suzy West

MATERIALS:

- One 8" x 12" and one 4" x 8" Canvas - *Canvas Concepts*
- White paint - *Plaid* Folk Art
- Patterned paper - *SEI*
- Tutu - *Target*
- Ballet shocs - *Encore*
- Pink Letters - *Making Memories*
- Scrappy Glue - *Magic Scraps*
- Adhesive - *Canvas Concepts*
- Flowers, tulle, staple gun

INSTRUCTIONS:

1. Paint all of small canvas. Paint the edges of the large canvas.
2. Print the words "I hope you" on patterned paper.
3. Cut the paper to fit the small canvas.
4. Add Pink letters to spell out "dance".
5. Wrap Tulle over the whole canvas and staple it to the back side.
6. Glue or staple the ballet slippers to the canvas.
7. Adhere photo to the large canvas.
8. Put tutu on canvas.
9. Staple the tutu to the back of the canvas.

1. Adhere printed words onto canvas.

2. Adhere letters onto title strip.

3. Wrap tulle over canvas and staple to the back side.

4. Staple ballet shoes and tulle to the front of canvas.

5. Adhere photo to the large canvas.

6. Staple the tutu to the back of the canvas.

My friends have made the story of my life.
-Helen Keller

I am lucky to have such great friends.

May we laugh, cry and create memories

together for the rest of our lives.
♥Krista

girlfriends g girlfriends

Hardware

The gratitude we feel when we are blessed with friends holds this book together as much as the hinges and velcro.

A small booklet comes out of the niche to reveal photos and more quotations, while the opposite canvas presents the sentiment, "I am lucky to have such great friends. May we laugh, cry, and create memories together for the rest of our lives."

This canvas book provides a fresh response to that constant question, "What unique, fun gift can I give my life-long best friend for her birthday?"

This idea can be extended for other occasions as well. Just change the colors and quotes to fit your theme.

Girlfriends
by Krista Fernandez

MATERIALS:

- Two 6" x 6" Canvases - *Canvas Concepts*
- Bubblegum paint - *Plaid*
- Icicle patterned paper - *KI Memories*
- Cardstock (Pink, Green) - *Bazzill*
- 2 hinges - *Canvas Concepts*
- Ribbon - *Offray, SEI*
- Girls are Weird font - *www.pixilated.com*
- Blooms, ball chain, button, brads, eyelets - *Making Memories*
- Photo Tape - *3L*
- Glue Dots - *Glue Dots International*
- Narrow rick-rack, Velcro circle, staple gun, eyelet tools, hammer

INSTRUCTIONS:

1. Paint the front and sides of one canvas and the sides only of a second canvas with Bubblegum. Let dry.
2. Cut a 6" x 6" cardstock and collage it with patterned papers, ribbons, flowers, and text as desired. Adhere the cover to the sides-only painted canvas. Also, cover the inside of this canvas with a 6" square of Pink and a 3¾" square of "Circles" paper.
3. Print sentiments on Pink cardstock and adhere them over the "Circles" paper with staples. Add ribbons and rick-rack.
4. For the other canvas, cut a 6" square from Pink paper. Cut out a 2½" square window so the canvas has a niche. Cut 4 strips of "Circles" paper ¾" x 3¾". Glue the strips around the window of the Pink paper and set it aside.
5. Staple a 10" ribbon in place referring to photo #2. Wrap the ribbon around the back of the canvas.
6. Adhere the framed window paper to the canvas, hiding the end of the ribbon.
7. Put the insides of the book together. Turn the canvases on their sides. Add the hinges ¾" from each end.
8. Adhere the Velcro to the front of the book and end of the ribbon.
9. To make the mini-book, cut cardstock squares 2⅜". Set an eyelet in the upper left corner of each square.
10. Thread a ball chain through the eyelets. Tie ribbons around the chain.
11. Decorate the pages with photos of friends and your favorite embellishments.
12. Place the mini-book in the niche.

1. Paint the canvases Pink.

2. Attach the ribbon.

3. Attach the Velcro.

Mini Portfolio

by Emelyn Magpoc

MATERIALS:

- Two 4" x 4" Canvases and one 4" x 8" Canvas - *Canvas Concepts*
- Ballet Pink paint - *Plaid* Folk Art
- Check fabric and flowers - Scrapaddict.com
- 2 hinges - *Canvas Concepts*
- Leather tie ups - *Nostalgiques*
- Photo Tape - *3L*
- Beads, leaf, hot glue gun

INSTRUCTIONS:

1. Paint all surfaces of all 3 canvases with Ballet Pink.
2. Attach hinges.
3. Rip the Check fabric into two 4" squares.
4. Adhere fabric to the canvas with Photo Tape.
5. Cut an "M" from fabric.
6. Tie a strip of scrap fabric to the "M".
7. Adhere the "M" to the canvas with hot glue.
8. Hot glue the leaf, flowers and beads in place.
9. Add string ties to the front of the canvases.
10. Adhere photos inside the canvas with Photo Tape.

1. Paint the canvases Pink.

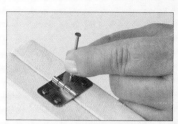

2. Hinge the canvases together.

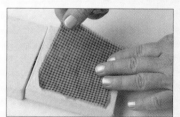

3. Tape fabric to canvas.

4. Stick closures in place.

5. Tape photos inside.

Mixed Media

A memory book is a thoughtful gift for a family member anytime, but especially when someone is moving away from home. Keep this project in mind next time you need a graduation or "moving to a new job" gift for a friend or loved one. It is a touching reminder of how much they are loved.

This "M" book is particularly enjoyable to look at and hold because of the variety of textures it provides the viewer. Metal, leather and waxed linen secure the closure while fabric, silk and beads decorate the covers that open to reveal enthusiastic photos of a loving family.

Made with small canvases, this art fits easily on a desk or computer monitor where it can be enjoyed daily.